**know the game**

Sea Angling

by Michael Prichard, A.R.P.S.

produced in collaboration with

THE NATIONAL FEDERATION OF SEA ANGLERS

Contents

FOREWORD

Since time immemorial old and young alike have gone to the sea to fish, either from the beaches, piers or from boats.

In 1904 a number of thinking people decided to start a Federation for the purpose of bringing sea anglers together in friendly rivalry, hence the competitions as we know them today.

Two other objects decided at that time were to make rules governing the sport of Sea Angling, particularly in Festivals and Competitions of all kinds, also to watch commercial sea fisheries of the British Isles and all matters relating thereto and to make representations in the interest of sea anglers to the appropriate authorities.

From that small beginning the Federation has now grown to the most influential sea anglers' association in Britain.

Membership of the Federation is either at Club level or through Personal Membership details of which are obtainable from our Secretary Mr. R. W. Page, 26 Downsview Crescent, Uckfield, Sussex TN22 1UB.

D. R. HALES
Chairman
National Federation of Sea Anglers

Introduction

Sea angling is both the newest and fastest growing aspect of the sport of fishing. Less than a hundred years old, it grew out of the commercial form of fishing known as long-lining . . . fishing with a long length of line to which were attached upwards of a hundred hooks. Men, living near to the sea, augmented the family diet by fishing with a handline either from a boat or cast, using a casting stick, from the shore. Success in providing for the family table encouraged fishers to experiment with both lighter gear and such sophisticated accessories as a reel on which to store their line and a rod to give sensitivity and add a sense of the thrill of the fight to their labours. So, sea angling as a sport was born.

It took a long time for the tackle to resemble that which we use today. Because sea fishing gear had to withstand considerable pressures; both from the size of the fish and from the tidal conditions prevailing, both rods and reels were cumbersome items generally made from natural materials such as wood and bamboo cane. As freshwater rods were lightened so the manufacturing techniques developed within the rod industry were applied to sea angling rods. From whole cane we moved to split cane, sometimes reinforced by a steel core, this move gave a lighter rod but they were still far too stiff to give a satisfactory feel when playing any but the largest of sea fish. A new dimension, in sea angling tackle, came with the introduction of fibre glass and the techniques necessary to extrude solid glass rods or hollow glass tubes. Here was a material unaffected by salt and the inevitable corrosion, light in weight and yet having immense strength.

The choice of a rod, in either hollow or solid glass, in the 1970s is really one of price. Solid glass rods are generally cheaper and for most boat fishing will perform well and cover many of the types of angling undertaken. Fishing from the shore involves casting tackle and bait out into the sea and here we find that the demand is for rods made in hollow glass. They cast better because they have more action built into them and are a lot lighter which is a must when the rod has to be held in one's hands during the fishing day.

It is not only the improvement in tackle and methods that have brought about the rapid growth of the sport, many anglers have turned to the sea because access to freshwater fishing has become increasingly difficult over the last few years together with a gradual decline in the quality of the available waters for coarse fishing. During the time of the foot and mouth epidemic, which swept the farmlands of Britain, rivers and lakes were closed to all forms of fishing which caused anglers to seek their leisure elsewhere! Probably the one factor that makes up an angler's mind when deciding on his chosen aspect of the sport is that fishing in the sea is free! There are very few areas around our coastline that are denied to the shore fisherman. According to time of year and the amount of money in his pocket there is and should be for all time fishing to suit everybody.

Whether one fishes from the shore or from a boat is a decision generally arrived at after consideration of the relative costs. The shore angler requires his tackle, bait and transport to the chosen venue, whilst a boat angler has to add the quite heavy expense of complete or part hiring of the angling boat. A day's boat fishing can be expensive but often produces either bigger fish or more fish than the shore fisher can muster. One thing is certain, boat fishing will become dearer as fuel charges, insurance, wages and boat purchase prices rise. Many anglers are thinking about owning their own boat, either a dinghy or perhaps part ownership of a larger craft as a group activity.

Shorecasting from the shingle at Flamborough Head, Yorkshire Coast. This part of the East Coast of Britain is known for good winter cod fishing.

Boat fishing out in Dingle Bay, Co. Kerry, produces a nice bull huss (Greater-Spotted Dogfish).

Whichever aspect of the sport you choose you will find that see angling offers a great deal . . . it is both healthy and relaxing . . . and fun. Whatever your age there is some form of sea fishing made for you because this is a wide horizoned sport . . . from shark to gobies, in the rock pools, enjoyed by peers and postmen alike.

The Sea Angler's Species

It would be difficult, within the pages of this new-comer's handbook, to discuss all the sea fish that inhabit the waters around our shores. There are over 400 of them but only a small number are of true angling importance. If we take fish in order of physical size first we must begin with the sharks. There are a number that are brought to us by the warm currents, of the Atlantic Ocean, during the summer. Shark fishers regularly catch two species, the blue and the porbeagle shark. Generally they are taken from the South and West coasts of Britain and Ireland, although one porbeagle has been landed on rod and line in Scottish waters in recent years. Tope and the various species of dogfish, all smaller members of the shark family, are of much greater importance to sea anglers as they can be caught through most months of the year and are found off most British coastal areas. Unlike the larger sharks, tope and dogfish move close inshore and are readily available to the shore angler.

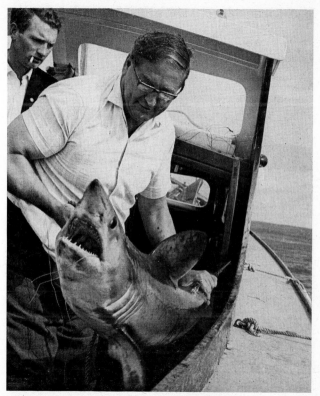

Leslie Moncrieff lifts a small porbeagle shark into the boat. Sharks of this size abound in the waters of Galway Bay.

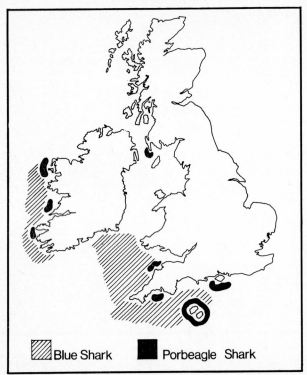

The shark fishing areas of Britain. Porbeagle areas are more specific from an angling point of view but many fish have been taken by commercial fishermen in other places, notably in Scotland and the North-East.

A strong, fighting tope is brought to the boat's side. Pound for pound, they are one of the sea angler's strongest fish.

Sharks are often called cartilaginous fish, like their close relatives the skates and rays they have a skeletal structure made of gristle often given further strength by a calcium-like deposit. None of this group of fishes have bones in the true sense.

The largest group of fishes, found in both fresh and saltwater, are the bony fishes having a complete skeleton similar to animals and man. This group of fish, numbering many thousands, vary tremendously in size. From the tiny tropical species kept in home aquariums to the massive halibut taken by distant water trawlers from Arctic seas.

One of the larger members of the cod family, the ling is taken over reefs and wrecks in deep water.

This kind of day's fishing puts a fantastic strain on sea angling gear and end tackles . . . five huge common skate taken during one of the Westport Festivals.

From an angling point of view the cod family must rank first in order of merit, closely followed by the flat fish. To these fish, the shore angler must add the bass and mullet whilst boat fishers have the conger eel and sea breams as additional quarry. There are, of course, many other species of sea fish to be found and caught in British waters, but most of them are taken accidently whilst fishing for other species. Although sea fishermen have developed methods and techniques suitable for catching the main angling fish, these methods are not discriminatory and will be found equally suitable for taking other minor species. There is a certain amount of control allied to using particular baits, such as squid for cod or even metal pirks for the cod family, but even then lesser known

7

fish will take the offered lure. Any successful angler will tell you that to catch fish one has to present a bait or lure in a manner likely to attract the fish and stimulate their feeding instinct. As all sea fish are predators, willing to feed on lesser brethren, of a different species or smaller specimens of their own species, a properly presented bait or lure will hook almost anything!

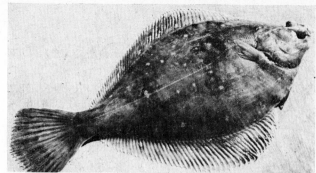

The plaice, it has vivid orange spots which persist in colour after the fish has been out of water for a long time.

Very different in appearance but all members of the cod family.
Top. The coalfish.
Centre The haddock
Bottom. The cod

Gaffing a conger eel into the boat. This eel is incredibly strong and often dives for the security of tangled wreckage or rocks after taking a bait. Your tackle has to be able to take the strain of a prolonged fight when conger fishing!

One of the more colourful species, the red sea bream, that come to our waters in the summer.

A pirk, made from plated metal and given a 'banana shape' to make it work in the water. Fished for a variety of species in deep water over wrecks or reefs.

Habitat has a great deal to do with which species of fish any fisher can expect to catch. From the shore, you should make an effort to inspect the fishing situation at low water. The area of ground uncovered by a really low tide will always tell a story. It may be that such an inspection will show a worm bed or beds of shellfish, such as mussel. Perhaps there will be a number of rocks uncovered by the tide, with weed growth ideal for providing a home for the many small crabs of the littoral waters. As the tide returns so fish will follow eager to find these pockets of food. Present a hook bait in these places and you fish with more than an even chance of meeting a hungry fish. It is wrong to assume that all sea areas have fish living and feeding within them. There is no even spread of fish population throughout our seas.

Always a good sight . . . the shore at low water. A close inspection will give you a clue to the whereabouts of fish when the tide returns and covers the weed, rock and shellfish.

Like animals, fish live or move to areas capable of supporting them as a life form. They require two things; food to sustain them as individuals and as a species together with a secure place in which to exist and breed.

Any obstruction to the flow of tide, a pier, harbour wall, outcrop of rock or wreck will enable plants and small animals to live. These obstructions then provide both a larder, constantly replenished by Nature, and places in which to hide or from which to ambush smaller fish or feed animals.

Boat anglers will look for similar situations but in deeper water. They will not be able to see the habitat in which the fish live, but by using charts giving soundings of the depth and having underwater obstructions marked they are able to determine where fish ought to live. The skippers that run sea angling charter boats will also be a mine of information on where they have been most successful in past ventures. The boat skipper is often the key to a good day's fishing . . . he's had lots of experience and his living depends on producing fish for his customers. Membership of a fishing club will also bring to a new fisherman a lot of information and advice on where and how to fish. Sometimes it is not necessary to ask how or where, just watch what the successful angler does and try to reason why.

A charter boat sits on an oily sea at anchor. Not always the best conditions in which to catch fish, a little more movement of tide will bring feed and encourage fish to take a bait.

Tackling up for shore fishing

First you need a rod and a reel, the size and type of rod depends more on the method of fishing than on the species you expect or hope to catch! Basically, a shore angler casts a bait out into the water. It is carried out by a lead and it is the size of this lead that determines the type of beachcasting rod. Most anglers fishing in the winter hope to catch cod and the conditions of wind and tide more often than not call for a reasonably heavy lead to take a large bait out and tether it securely on the bottom. With leads of around 6 ounces the traditional rod is one of twelve feet in length, made of fibre glass. On some occasions the current flow will require the use of a lead with wire grips that dig into the sand or shingle giving a more secure hold thus preventing the bait from rolling round in the current. This lead has to be brought back from time to time to inspect the bait or perhaps to land a fish. Retrieving a heavy lead, with or without grip wire places a heavy strain upon the rod so demanding that the rod has sufficient **backbone** to cope with the strain. Long, stronger rods can also cast further than lighter ones. Much has been said and written about the ability to cast great distances. And, although it is not always necessary to cast a bait prodigious distances it can be the only way to catch fish at times. When there are a number of fishermen on a beach, all hurling leads out so often it is the man that is able to cast furthest that catches what is there. A number of leads hitting the surface of the water at round about the same distance will often drive fish further out

The beachcasting rod in action. Leslie Moncrieff, the 'Father', of modern shore fishing techniques, casts out from the shingle at Dungeness.

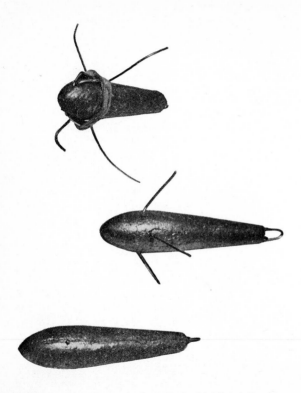

to the quieter ground and any bait that arrives there may do the trick!

Fishing closer in for smaller species in slacker water conditions can call for a light rod, certainly bass fishers in the West and men fishing for flats in an estuary often use small baits and light leads with rods suitable for freshwater fishing! Many species, bass, mullet, wrasse and pollack can be fished for using a float and very light gear because the fishing is close to the rocks or into a harbour wall which does not necessitate using a lead to achieve fishing distance. Spinning, with an artificial lure, such as is done in many freshwater situations, calls for a rod that could well be used for salmon or pike.

Three different shorecasting leads: L-R.A rubber band, breakaway grip lead; the conventional grip lead with fixed stiff wires and plain casting torpedo lead.

The bass, a popular beach fisherman's fish from the surf beaches. A superb, hard fighter, with beautiful scaling and spines on the first dorsal fin and gill case.

The ballan wrasse, seek this hard fighter around the rocky shelf that has deep water close in.

Just the place to fish into deep water without having to cast long distances. Piers and harbour walls can yield very good fish that come close into the shore to seek feed that lives on the piling or is thrown into the harbour by man.

There are two types of shore fishing reels—the multiplier and the fixed-spool. Both are equally successful and their use is purely a matter of individual choice. For a

The multiplying and fixed-spool reel.
A. Bale arm
B. Bale arm roller—keep this free from dirt and salt encrustation.
C. Drag knob—gives fine adjustment of the slipping spool.
D. Anti-reverse lever.
E. Free-spool lever.
F. Ratchet on/off button.
G. Star drab wheel—gives fine adjustment of the slipping tension.
H. Spindle bearing adjustment screw.

The moment of release as the rod comes to full compression building the power to throw the lead out beyond the third breaker, where the bass may be waiting?

newcomer to casting, the fixed-spool reel is certainly easier to use particularly at night when the line running off the spool cannot easily be seen or controlled. To cast the bail arm is opened and the line picked up onto the index finger. The cast is made with the finger releasing the line as the compression built up in the rod drives the lead forward. The line runs freely off the spool and when the lead is seen to hit the water and settle, the handle of the reel is turned which automatically closes the bail arm again. The fixed-spool reel can be used in all forms of shore fishing-beachcasting, spinning and float fishing and has only one major problem in use. That is that as the line has to be held across the joint of the index finger, a strong cast with a heavy lead can cause the line to cut into the finger. At least one tackle company has produced a casting release mechanism that prevents this damage to an angler's hand. It is said that a fixed-spool is difficult to control as the line runs off but as over half of British shore fishermen use the reel it cannot be too much of a fault!

On the other hand, multiplying reels can be controlled but they demand more than a modicum of skill in their use. The principle is that the reel has a freely-running spool that can be disengaged, at the moment of casting, allowing line to peel off the spool as it revolves. Naturally, the turning of the spool has to be stopped, as the lead slows in flight, or it will continue to revolve resulting in a 'Bird's Nest' of loose coils. Some reels are supplied having a built-in braking system that is claimed to prevent this happening. The only certain way to ensure a trouble free casting day is to learn to cast well and smoothly.

Nearly all shore fishers use nylon monofilament line, it's cheap and flows freely from the spool when casting. Breaking strains vary as the diameter of the line increases but the following strengths of line should suit most shore angling—

Heavy shore fishing	6 oz. lead 40 lb. leader	18—25 lb. reel line
Light shore fishing	3 oz. lead 30 lb. leader	12—15 lb. reel line
Spinning (lure to 1 oz.)		8—12 lb. reel line
Float fishing (depending on species fished for)		8—12 lb. reel line

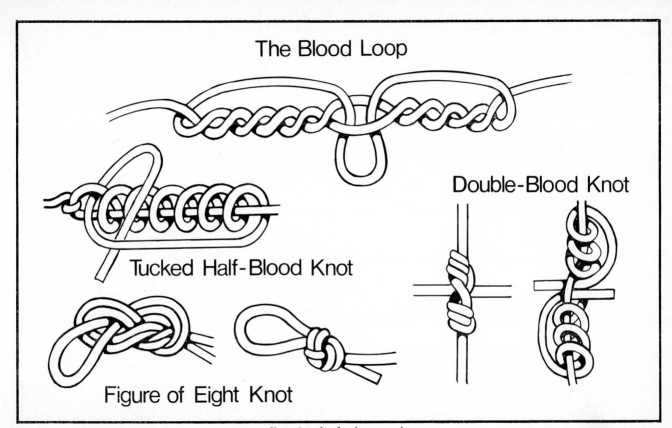

The Blood Loop

Double-Blood Knot

Tucked Half-Blood Knot

Figure of Eight Knot

Knots in nylon for the sea angler.

Two factors must be explained when choosing your reel line—

(a) The leader is a length of heavier gauge nylon blood knotted onto the reel line to absorb the shock of casting a heavy lead. It also serves to give added strength to the line when the fish is close into the shore and a strong sea may cause a sudden strain such as would break the reel line. About twenty feet of leader will suffice.

(b) Fishing from a harbour wall or from a pier will call for a heavier reel line because the fish has to be brought in close and then lifted vertically placing an exceptional strain on your tackle. It is wise to either raise the breaking strain to take this factor into account or invest in a drop net, that can be lowered down to the fish to secure it and relieve the strain on the reel line.

A 'Mustad' split link, useful for attaching shorecasting rigs to the casting leader or for joining two pieces of nylon. They are immensely strong and will not break when casting heavy gear on a crowded beach.

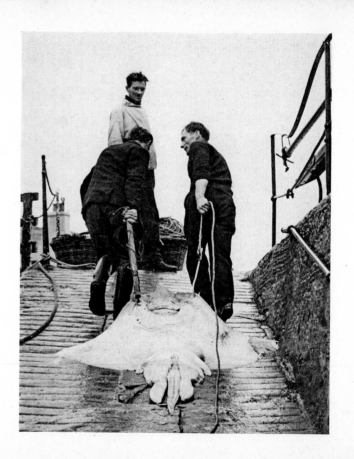

Shore fishing rigs

There are just two basic shore fishing rigs for casting and fishing a legered bait. The nylon paternoster and the running leger are both simple to form and must be simple in use. Too often we see complicated rigs, using metal booms and other pieces of ironmongery, that can only lead to problems when fishing. A simple rig will lessen the chance of getting hooked up in the bottom and will be easier cast out. Furthermore, complicated rigs must inevitably cost more money to use and to lose!

A simple nylon paternoster for most beach fishing situations, made from a 4 foot length of nylon having the same breaking strain as the casting leader. Tie in split links, for attachment of lead and casting leader, at each end, Blood loops should be formed, in the paternoster, to take hook droppers. Tie short droppers, using the same breaking strain of nylon as used on the reel, to the hooks, using a tucked-half blood knot and forming loops with an overhand knot.

A rig for fish that run off with a bait . . . the nylon running leger. A three foot length of nylon of about the same breaking strain as the reel line. Tie on the hook, using a tucked-half-blood knot with a loop for attachment to the link swivel. The lead runs on the casting leader, the bead stops the lead loop from jamming on to the split link or link swivel.

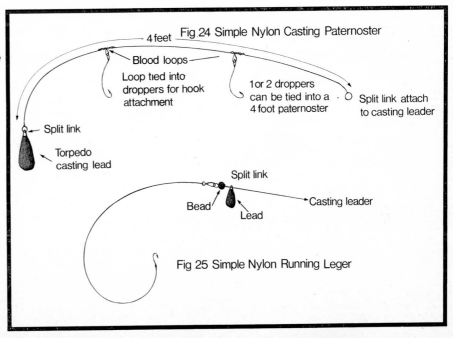

4 feet — Fig 24 Simple Nylon Casting Paternoster

Blood loops

Loop tied into droppers for hook attachment

1 or 2 droppers can be tied into a 4 foot paternoster

Split link attach to casting leader

Split link

Torpedo casting lead

Split link

Bead

Casting leader

Lead

Fig 25 Simple Nylon Running Leger

A note of warning . . . beware of casting on crowded beaches, make sure that all your knots are secure and that swivels, joining lines together, are robust enough to take the shock of casting. They are fine when under the strain of playing a fish . . . which is a constant pressure, but can fail under a sudden snatch load. Better to use a simple split ring as a link between lines.

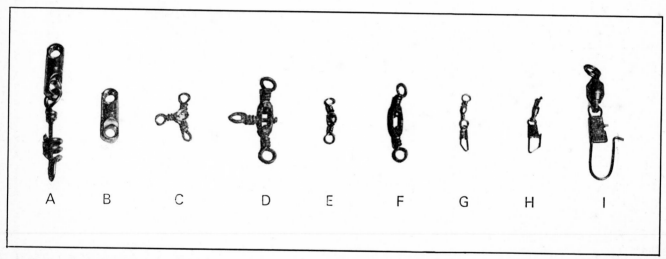

A selection of swivels used by sea anglers.
A. Heavy duty swivel with corkshrew link
B. Plain heavy duty swivel
C. Three-way swivel
D. Heavy duty three-way box swivel
E. Barrel swivel
F. Box swivel
G. Barrel link swivel
H & I. Ball-bearing link swivels

Both the paternoster and running leger can be made using wire lines to the hooks, so often necessary when the fish have sharp teeth or grinding teeth, as in the case of the tope, dogfish and rays. Fine cable-laid wire can be knotted to form hook links or loops but heavier gauges, of 30—60 lbs. will require crimping with ferrules using the fixing methods shown.

All float fishing rigs are a variation on the rig illustrated and only really vary when the depth of water is such that a sliding float rig is called for. A simple clove hitch, around a small piece of rubber band, will stop the float at the required depth but allow the line to be wound back onto the reel spool with the float stop moving freely through the rod rings. Spinning rigs are simple, just a piece of heavier gauge nylon or perhaps flexible wire with a snap link swivel to aid attachment of the lure. Some species that are caught spinning do have sharp teeth and may bite through the spinning line.

The simplest form of attaching wire to both hook and swivel to make a wire trace. This material is vital when fishing for skate, conger and other fish with sharp teeth.

19

Float Fishing Rig

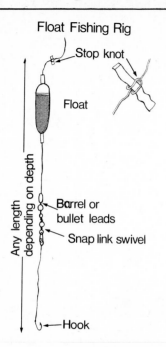

Stop knot

Float

Any length depending on depth

Barrel or bullet leads

Snap link swivel

Hook

A standard float rig for the shore angler. Use a cork or balsa-bodied float capable of carrying a wide range of leads because of the variation in the size of the various baits to be fished. A large float, well leaded will assist when making long casts particularly into strong winds.

Spinning Trace

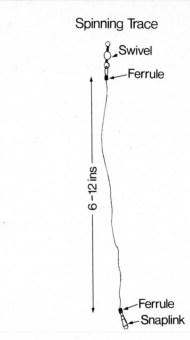

Swivel

Ferrule

6–12 ins

Ferrule

Snaplink

A simple spinning trace can be constructed, in any length, from nylon covered wire crimping a loop at one end, around the reel line swivel, and a snap link to enable easy removal and changing of your lures.

Always pay a great attention to the quality and sharpness of your hooks, they are, after all, the most important part of your tackle. Try to keep them free of rust and separate, hooks that rattle about in a tin or plastic box will gradually lose their points and erode the points of the barbs and may lose a good fish. Choose a hook that is of the right size to accommodate the bait. Too small a hook may mean that your strike will pull the hook out of the fish's mouth without taking hold, too large a hook and a shy-biting fish will feel the hook too readily and spit the bait out. It is a question of compromise between hook size, bait size and fish species. Some fish, flatfish particularly, have extremely small mouths for their body size. It is difficult to remove a hook with a normal shank size, use a long-shanked hook that you can get a hold on.

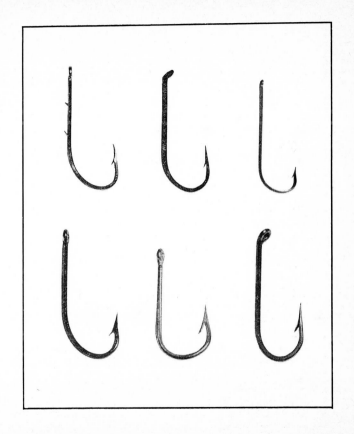

A selection of hooks for the sea angler—Left to right,
Bottom: *O'Shaughnessy, forged hook for general boat fishing*
          Mustad 'Seamaster', forged with brazed eye for heavy
            duty work
          Stainless steel, 'Model Perfect', for heavy boat fishing
Top: *Mustad Beak hook, with sliced shank, a popular hook*
          for all purposes
          Fine wire, 'Model Perfec' for the shore angler
          'Cannelle', fine wire hook for the light tackle beach
            fisherman

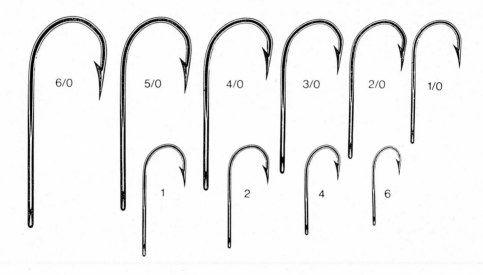

Hook relative sizes: 6/0 *for big fish, such as cod, ling and conger.*
3/0 *for codling, bass, whiting and pollack.*
2—6 *for wrasse, flatfish and other small species.*

Detecting a bite

There are two ways in which the bite of a fish are brought to the angler's notice; a visual signal when the rod is placed in a rod rest or leaned against a wall or railing. The rod tip will tremble, it may give a pronounced movement or even a thumping downward pull. If this happens and you are near enough to grab the rod and strike you may well hook and land the fish. Then there is the bite communicated through the angler's fingers, as a variety of vibrations or pulls on the line. No two fish species give the same bite, in fact there is a tremendous variation in bites from the same species depending upon the strength of the tidal stream, the bait in use and how the fish are feeding. Nobody can say with authority that this or that fish bites in a particular and specific fashion. The important thing is to be able to recognise a bite when you get one! Always hold your rod if you can. More fish steal the bait and get away unhooked because the angler is away from his rod than are lost because of tackle breakages or angling inexperience!

Some species, and here I can suggest the flatfish, have a habit of taking a bait slowly. They seem to pull the bait about and this is seen as a tremble on the rod tip or felt as a series of tweaks on the reel line. If you do strike immediately the first pull is felt you may not hook the fish, they need time to get the bait into their mouths. You will not know, at first, that the bites are from flatfish but the experience of having this type of bite and losing then hooking a few will soon sort out your individual angling style . . . It is incredibly difficult to convey to anyone what a bite feels like and how it feels to hook and play a fish. But, once anybody has had the first experience of the bite followed by the playing of a fish they know just what it is all about!

Landing a fish from the shore

Apart from the moment of hooking your fish this can be the most critical time of the fight. Should a large wave happen along just as the fish is in shallow water or about

This is the time to take care, a bass fights desperately to break away. Given the slightest amount of slack line and it will be off back into the breakers!

to be lifted up onto a rack platform it can catch the angler unawares, place a sudden stress on the hook hold and and away tears the hook resulting in a lost specimen. Try to play a fish out before beaching it . . . let the swell lift it into the shore then move smartly to take hold of it before the next wave either removes it or knocks you off your balance. The casting leader will give that added strength to the line at this important time.

Baits for the shore angler

As I said earlier, fish are predators on almost everything that lives in the sea but not all this food is available as bait for the angler to either buy or collect. Worms, the lugworm and ragworm, are probably the universal bait with fish, such as mackerel, sprat and herring almost as good. Many of the smaller invertebrates, shellfish, crabs in the peeler stage and squids are also among the baits that form the mainstay of angling. Apart from bait that can be bought from the tackle shop or fishmonger an angler must come to recognise what a worm bed looks like and having found it learn to dig for himself. Not only is bait expensive but one gets a kick out of digging bait then catching a fish on it! Try to present the bait in a natural fashion. Thread worms onto the hook so that they retain their shape, I do not suggest that fish will not take a hotchpotch of bait, crudely strung onto the hook, but I feel that more bites ensue if the offering looks life-like. This feeling applies particularly to fish bait where a shapeless lump is so often ignored, whereas a fillet cut to resemble a small fish is readily taken.

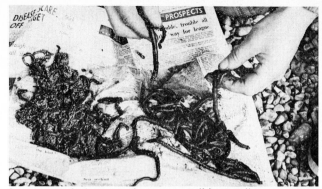

Sorting over the lugworm, these worms will keep well if individually wrapped in clean newspaper.

Ragworms.

A sharp knife and steady hand are vital when cutting a lash of bait from the side of a herring or mackerel. Always use a cutting board and not the thwarts of somebody else's boat!

Digging for lugworm on an empty Welsh beach.

Tackling up for boat fishing

Boat fishing rods are generally shorter than shore rods, they have to be! Firstly, they are not used to cast with as boat angling means lowering the bait to the sea bed and secondly, long rods would be too unwieldy to handle in the confines of an open cockpit. There are many kinds of boat rod, from the ultra-strong rod meant to cope with fish of over a thousand pounds down to the ultra-light rod used when fishing from a dinghy for flounders or other small inshore fish. What you need is just a case of balancing the gear to the type of species found in your sea area.

Present as lively a bait as possible—take the hook through the strip, give it a twist and hook through once more which will give it action in the water!

Manufacturers now relate the power of a rod to a definite breaking strain of line which gives the modern angler a better yardstick when choosing his rod. Let us take a situation and match our gear to it. Fishing from a south of England port having a fairly strong tide stream at certain times of the year. The fish present could be cod, in the winter, with whiting and pouting. Some inshore flatfish, plaice and the occasional turbot, with tope and small rays during the summer months. This is very much a general picture for a large proportion of the country's inshore waters. If we assume that leads of up to 1 lb. may at times be necessary and most of the fishing is done from an anchored boat, a rod capable of handling lines from 25—40 lbs. would be right. This type of rod is often referred to as a general purpose one. Most tackle companies have such a rod and it could cope with both the conditions and the various species name above.

Two boat rods in action, both are 7 feet long with sufficient rings to distribute the strains of playing heavy fish, evenly along the rod blanks.

Off for a day's dinghy fishing in an Essex estuary. A twelve footer, capable of carrying two anglers and their gear with a safety margin.

There are, as with the shore equipment, two reels that one could use: a boat multiplier used above the rod or a centre-pin reel that hangs below the rod. There are advantages and disadvantages with both types. The multiplier is smaller and has a slipping clutch mechanism, this allows a strong fish to take line off the reel at a fixed slipping tension before the breaking strain of the line is reached. Unfortunately most of them have a low rate of

A boat fishing multiplying reel. With a metal, anodised alloy spool to resist corrosion. Robust and having a capacity for 300 yards of 30 lb. nylon or braided line. Gear ratio is one turn of the handle to three turns of the spool.

retrieve. The centre-pin is a direct-drive reel without the gearing found in the multiplier. It has a much greater recovery of line as it uses a much larger drum or spool on which the line is carried. The main problem, with some of them, is that they have no slipping clutch and a powerful fish can rip line off the reel, causing the handles to revolve at tremendous speed. Should an angler attempt to arrest the downward plunge of the fish, by grabbing the handles, he may well get his fingers badly bruised or worse! One thing is vital in both reels and that is that they must have a spool constructed from an un-crushable material. Nylon line, wound on under great pressure as when playing a heavy fish in a strong tide run, can create a fantastic pressure on any spool . . . sufficient to explode the plastic or lightweight spools found on shore fishing multipliers.

The boat fisherman has a wider choice of reel line . . . nylon for most fishing is more than adequate but it tends to stretch, some of them up to 10% of the overall length. There is then some loss of sensitivity in the hooking and playing of the fish. Light tackle anglers and those that fish for the huge specimens of the sea have moved towards braided Terylene or Dacron lines. They have little stretch but are considerably more expensive to buy. In addition, more care has to be taken of them when fishing as they are prone to abrasion, either on underwater obstructions or the boat, which severely cuts down the line strength. Then there is wire line, in a number of differing forms. Either as single strand, a few twisted strands or multi-braided strands this line has found favour with fishermen that have extra-strong tides to contend with. The wire is thinner than nylon or Dacron and has a certain amount of weight in itself thus making it easier to cut tide and get down into the water.

The boat fisherman tends to use far more metal in his forming of fishing rigs, swivels, booms and other items play a greater role in his tackle box. Some are necessary but I hasten to say that the simpler the tackle and rigs are the better they work and the less tangles you will have to sort out. We all get into a tangle, especially when fishing at anchor from a crowded charter boat, but some fishers seem unable to lower a bait unless it is accompanied by half a tackle shop!

Again, the type and condition of hooks is vitally important. They must be both sharp and of a quality capable of withstanding the heavy loads that they are expected to bring to the surface. It is a false economy to buy cheap hooks when one considers the all-over price of any day's boat fishing!

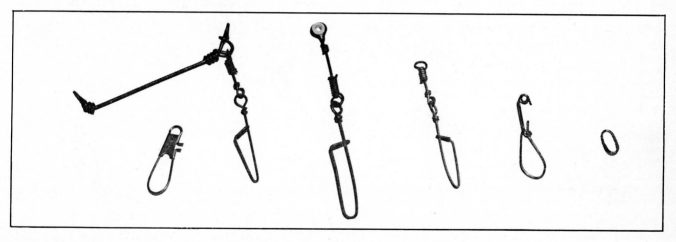

A sea angler's ironmongery! Left to right: *Stainless steel snap link, used on the reel line to attach traces, etc.*
Clement's boom, to run on the line and carry the lead weight.
Kilmore boom, has a porcelain eye to ensure free-running on the line.
Simple, twisted wire, lead attaching link.
Another variation, cheap and simple.
A Mustad split link for the shore caster.

Baits for the boat fisher

All of the baits discussed in the shore angling section can be used by a boat fisherman. In addition, a wide range of artificial lures, called pirks, have lately come into use. They are brightly painted or plated pieces of metal, sometimes resembling a fish but more often just relying on shape to impart the action of a small fish. Most members of the cod family will strike at them as will tope and the dogfish. They are not intended to be lowered to the sea bed and left as bait, rather they must be made to work. Having found bottom the angler must then work them, by a raising and lowering of the rod top, in such a way as to give this chunk of metal life.

Some spinning can be done from a boat, but not a crowded one! Species like bass and mackerel give great sport on light spinning gear and are ideal quarry for the dinghy fisher that works in estuaries and calm waters around reefs. Mackerel is regarded as one of the best of baits but too little could be caught using a spinner from a boat. Added to which, the other anglers aboard would be loath to wait while one of their number caught his bait in the **sporting fashion.** So strings of feathers are used to gather mackerel.

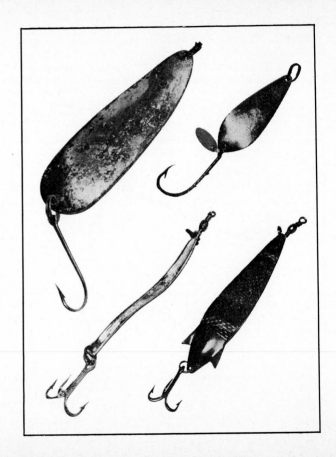

A variety of metal lures. The two at the top can be used with single hooks as flashers when boat fishing with bait or with treble hooks when spinning in a conventional fashion.

Basically, they are hooks, usually six on a six foot trace, tied with chicken feather covering the hook. In the water the feathered hooks simulate the actions of a shoal of tiny fry. Other fish can be taken with these attractors but is generally considered unsporting to fish seriously with this type of lure. A departure from the rule would be the use of single or two cod feathers sometimes baited with a sliver of fish of a single lugworm to give the feather a smell. Although varying sizes of fish

A three hook mackerel trace, any number of feathers can be tied onto the nylon trace but over six becomes unmanageable.

Feathering for mackerel bait, beware of swinging the fish on to the deck as you can easily hook yourself or another angler!

will all take similar sized baits it is usual to relate the size of bait to the fish you think are present and for which you are directing your fishing effort. So if the intention is to fish big use a big bait! Come to know something of the feed that different species eat and bait accordingly . . . whole skelps of mackerel for tope and skate, smaller lashes for cod and thin strips for bream and turbot, Worms for the flatfish other than the turbot and brill with a **mixed grill** or cocktail of both for the big winter cod. And, when fish bait is easier to come by in the summer, take home the remainder to store for the winter in the deep freeze. Bait is becoming a problem to find during the late months of the year.

Rigs for the boat angler

As with the shore fisher's rigs, the boat angler needs two basic tackles with perhaps a few subtle combinations and variations on them. The nylon paternoster is favourite although some people like to make the hook droppers stand off the trace line by using booms of metal or wire. The number of hooks used is up to you, two or three would be about right. When fishing certain species, cod, pollack, coalfish or ling, the addition of metal flashers tied onto the hook links will often raise the number of bites you get. It seems that anything resembling small fish or having movement cause these species to attack.

Paternosters are rigs that suspend the bait above the sea bed, they are most suitable for fish that swim and feed slightly off the bottom. When fish are scarce or you are experimenting to find what species are present it is better to combine the paternoster with a running leger rig to enable presentation of baits to both bottom feeding and above ground swimming fish. The only problem is that small species, such as pouting, will all too often give bites, are struck and the line retrieved before larger ground fish can see or take the legered bait, that is a thing that has to be put up with.

The running leger is a rig suitable for a vast number of our sea species. It is simple and can be adapted for most situations and sizes of fish from the minute dab to the massive common skate. Though intended for a single hook bait, multi-hook legers can be tied using nylon or wire traces. Remember that to be successful the legered

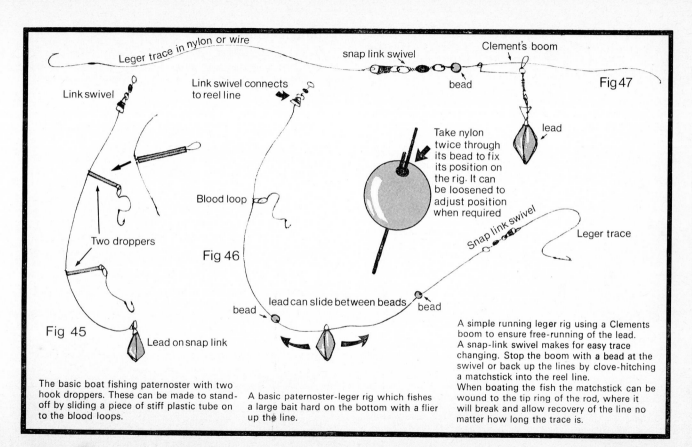

Leger trace in nylon or wire

snap link swivel

Clement's boom

Link swivel

Link swivel connects to reel line

bead

Fig 47

lead

Take nylon twice through its bead to fix its position on the rig. It can be loosened to adjust position when required

Blood loop

Two droppers

Fig 46

Snap link swivel

Leger trace

bead

lead can slide between beads

bead

Fig 45

Lead on snap link

The basic boat fishing paternoster with two hook droppers. These can be made to stand-off by sliding a piece of stiff plastic tube on to the blood loops.

A basic paternoster-leger rig which fishes a large bait hard on the bottom with a flier up the line.

A simple running leger rig using a Clements boom to ensure free-running of the lead. A snap-link swivel makes for easy trace changing. Stop the boom with a bead at the swivel or back up the lines by clove-hitching a matchstick into the reel line. When boating the fish the matchstick can be wound to the tip ring of the rod, where it will break and allow recovery of the line no matter how long the trace is.

bait must be fished hard on the sea bed . . . it is no use losing contact with your lead so that it rises in the water . . . bottom-dwelling fish will not come up in the tide to find the bait. If you cannot feel the lead on the sea bed, feed out a small amount of line off the reel until you re-establish contact. If that doesn't work, reel in and replace the lead with a heavier one or lower the same gear and fish it until contact is lost and repeat the exercise.

If the running leger is to be used to advantage, the lead must slide without hindrance on the reel line so that fish can take the bait without feeling any resistance to their mouthing. A Clements or Kilmore boom give this free-sliding facility. Lower the rig slowly, in slack water, because there is a tendency for the hook length to twist back up the main line.

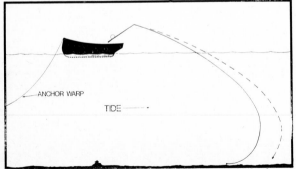

The line does not leave the rod tip and go down to the lead in a straight line, it adopts a curve (as shown). If you lose contact with the lead and allow line to run off the reel a large belly will form in the line making bites almost impossible to detect.

Bite detection from the boat

It can be a little more difficult to accurately discern bites when fishing from a boat. Firstly, there is the movement of the boat that lifts the lead from the sea bed in relation to the wave or swell pattern. Added to this, there is the problem of stretch when using nylon line tending to cancel out sudden movement of the lead or bait. Lastly, we have to contend with the different biting behaviour of the many species that can be encountered around the British Isles. Some species, such as the tope must be given time to pick up a bait, run off with it, turn the bait to swallow it before being struck. The skate and rays can be felt to flop on the bait striking the reel line with their snouts as they manoeuvre their mouths onto the bait. This is because their eyes are on the top of the body whilst their mouths are below which makes taking a bait a fairly slow operation to these fish. Fish with small mouths will pick at a bait, if it's too large, they whittle it down to a size that they can ingest. Fish with large mouths can grab and run but nevertheless one cannot lay down hard and fast rules as to biting behaviour.

Nothing can replace experience in an angler. One or two trips out with a number of different species caught each trip will lead the way to successful fishing for the future. It is not always necessary to catch fish to be able to enjoy a day's outing, but it is necessary to come to know why one didn't catch them. To analyse what happened, how the weather or sea conditions differed from other times or whether fish took different baits related to a change in the tide flow. All these factors affect the sport of sea fishing. If we knew why, where and how fish would bite on a regular basis it is doubtful whether the sport would have the pull on man that it does have. Remove the uncertainty of angling and you remove the appeal.

Safety and the sea angler

Never take chances with the sea . . . for it does not tolerate fools. All too often we read of anglers having to be rescued when out in small boats. Remember that to place yourself in a position from which you have to be rescued, either out in a small dinghy with a doubtful engine or from the base of cliffs that you cannot climb, you are asking somebody else to put their lives in jeopardy.

Take heed of weather forecasts and the advice of Coastguards before leaving the shore. Shore anglers must realise that the swell, out at sea, that presents no problem to a boat angler could well drive up onto the rock ledges and sweep them off with little chance of being recovered!

Equip your boat with the essential life support systems and insist that the party boat you book is similarly equipped. Wear sufficient clothing in bad weather to keep you both warm and dry, exposure can produce a severe chill. It is not true that a swig at the spirits bottle will ward off the cold, better that you take a flask of hot soup.

JOSEPH WARD & CO. (PRINTERS) LTD. DEWSBURY

National Federation of Sea Anglers / Regional Medal Sizes

AREA	A		B		C		D		E		F		G		I		H	
B BOAT S SHORE	**B**	**S**	**B**	**S**	**B**	**S**	**B**	**S**	**B**	**S**	**B**	**S**	**B**	**S**	**B**	**S**	**B**	**S**
ANGLER FISH	29	18	25	20	25	25	25	20	25	20	25	20	25	20	25	20	20	20
BASS	9½	9½	9½	9½	9½	9½	9½	9½	9½	9½	9½	9½	9½	9½	10	10	9½	9½
BREAM (BLACK)	4	2	4	2	4	2½	3½	2½	3½	2½	3½	2½	3½	2½	3	2	3	2
BREAM (RED)	4	1	3½	1	3½	1	3½	1	3	1	2	1	2	1	2	1	2	1
BRILL	4½	3¼	4½	3	6	3	5	3	5	3	4½	3	4½	3	4½	3	4	2½
BULL HUSS	14	12	15	12	15	10	14	8	14	8	13	8	16	8	13	8	12	6
COALFISH	16½	3½	14	3½	16	3½	12	3½	9	3	6	3	6	3	6	3	6	3
COD	23	9	18	9	23	9	23	10	24	15	24	15	26	18	23	12	23	13
DAB	1	1	1½	1	1½	1¼	1½	1	1½	1	1½	1¼	1½	1	1½	1	1	1
EEL (CONGER)	47	20	40	20	40	25	35	30	30	25	40	20	35	20	25	15	25	15
FLOUNDER	2	2	2	2	2¼	2¼	2½	2½	2½	2½	2½	2½	2½	2½	2½	2	2	2
GARFISH	1½	1½	1½	1½	1½	1½	1½	1½	1½	1½	1½	1¼	1½	1¼	1¼	1¼	1¼	1
GURNARD (TUB)	4	2½	3½	2½	3½	2½	3½	2½	3½	2½	3½	2½	3½	2½	3½	2	3	2
HADDOCK	5½	1	4	1	5½	1	4	1	4	1	4	1	3	1	3	1	5	1
JOHN DORY	4½	1	4½	1	4½	1	4½	1	3	1	3	1	3	1	3	1	3	1
LING	30	4½	25	4½	25	4½	20	5	15	5	15	5	12	5	12	5	12	5
MACKEREL	2	1¾	2	1¾	2	1¾	2	1¾	1¾	1¾	1¾	1¾	1¾	1½	1¾	1½	1½	1½
MONKFISH	35	25	35	25	35	25	35	25	35	25	35	25	35	25	35	25	30	20
MULLET (GREY)	4	4	4	4	4	4	4	4	4	4	4	4	4	4	4	4	4	4
PLAICE	3½	3¼	4	3¼	5	3½	4½	3¼	4	3	3½	3	4½	3	2¾	2	3¼	2½
POLLACK	16	5	16	6½	16	5	15	5	12	5	9	5	9	5	9	5	9	5
POUTING	3¼	1	3¼	1½	3¼	1½	3	1½	2½	1½	3¼	1¾	3¾	2¼	2½	1½	2½	1½
SCAD	1	1	1	1	1½	1	1½	1	1½	1	1½	1	1½	1	1½	1¼	1½	1
SHARK (BLUE)	80	–	80	–	80	–	50	–	40	–	40	–	40	–	40	–	40	–
SHARK (MAKO)	190	–	190	–	190	–	50	–	40	–	40	–	40	–	40	–	40	–
SHARK (POR-BEAGLE)	140	–	140	–	140	–	140	–	140	–	120	–	100	–	60	–	50	–
SHARK (THRESHER)	110	–	110	–	110	–	110	–	110		100	–	80	–	60	–	50	–
RAY (BLONDE)	16	5	15	5	20	5	25	8	20	8	20	8	15	5	12	5	12	5
RAY (STING)	28	24	25	20	25	20	25	20	25	20	25	20	25	20	30	20	25	20
RAY (SMALL EYED OR PAINTED)	12	5	11	5	11	6	11	6	11	6	8	6	8	6	8	5	8	5
RAY (THORN-BACK)	12	9	14	12	13	10	16	12	13	10	14	10	16	12	15	12	15	12
SMOOTHOUNDS	18	12	18	12	18	12	18	12	18	15	18	15	16	12	18	12	18	12
SPUR DOG	12	6½	10	8	10	8	14	8	12	8	12	8	12	8	12	8	12	8
SOLE	1¼	1½	1¾	1¾	1¾	1¾	2	2	2¼	2¼	2	2	2	2	2	2	2	5
TOPE	40	35	40	30	35	25	45	30	40	30	35	25	40	25	45	25	35	25
TURBOT	18	6½	19	7	19	7	19	6½	16	6	15	7	15	7	15	7	12	7
WEAVER	1	1	1	1	¾	¾	¾	¾	¾	¾	¾	¾	¾	¾	¾	¾	¾	¾
WHITING	3½	1½	3	1½	4	1¾	3½	1½	3½	1½	3½	1½	3½	2	3	2	3½	2
WRASSE	5	5	5	5	5	5	5	5	3½	3½	3½	3½	3	3	3½	3½	3	3

AREA	J		K		L		M		N		P		Q		R		S		T	
B BOAT S SHORE	**B**	**S**	**B**	**S**	**B**	**S**	**B**	**S**	**B**	**S**	**B**	**S**	**B**	**S**	**B**	**S**	**B**	**S**	**B**	**S**
ANGLER FISH	20	20	20	20	20	20	20	15	20	20	20	20	20	20	25	20	25	20	25	20
BASS	9½	7	9	7	9	9	9	7	9	9	9	9	9	9	9	9	9	9	10	10
BREAM (BLACK)	2½	2	2	1½	2½	2	2½	1½	2½	2	2½	2	2½	2	2½	2	3½	2½	3½	2¼
BREAM (RED)	2	1	2	1	2	1	2	1	2	1	2	1	2	1	2	1	2½	1	3½	1
BRILL	4	2½	4	2½	4	2	4	2½	4	2	4	2	4	2	4	2	4	2	5	3½
BULL HUSS	12	6	12	6	13	8	12	6	13	8	14	8	15	8	15	8	12	8	15	12
COALFISH	6	3	6	3	10	5	14	9	10	5	8	5	8	5	8	5	8	5	10	5
COD	22	12	22	15	15	10	22	10	15	10	15	10	16	10	18	12	18	12	22	12
DAB	1	1	1	1	1	1	1	1	1	1	1	1	1	1	1	1	1½	1	1½	1
EEL (CONGER)	20	10	20	10	25	20	35	25	25	20	25	15	25	10	25	15	35	25	35	25
FLOUNDER	1¾	1¾	1½	1½	2¼	2¼	1¾	1¾	2¼	2¼	2	2	2	2	2	2	2	2	2¾	2¾
GARFISH	1¼	1	1¼	1	1	1	1½	1½	1	1	1½	1	1½	1	1½	1	2	1½	1¾	1-6oz
GURNARD (TUB)	2	1½	1½	1½	5	5	3	3	5	5	5	5	5	5	5	3	4	3	5½	5½
HADDOCK	5	1	5	1	4	1	6	1	4	1	3	1	3	1	3	1	3	1	4	1
JOHN DORY	3	1	2	1	3	1	2	1	3	1	3	1	3	1	3	1	5	1	5	1
LING	12	5	12	5	15	5	15·	5	15	5	20	5	20	5	15	5	5	3	25	5
MACKEREL	1½	1½	1½	1½	1½	1½	2½	2	2	1½	2	1½	2	1½	2	1¾	2	1¾	2	1¾
MONKFISH	30	20	30	20	35	25	25	15	35	25	40	25	40	25	40	25	35	20	40	25
MULLET (GREY)	4	4	4	4	4	4	5	5	4	4	4	4	4	4	4	4	4	4	5	5
PLAICE	3¼	2½	3¼	2½	3½	2½	4	3	3½	2½	3½	2½	3½	3	3½	3	4	3½	5	3½
POLLACK	9	5	9	5	9	5	14	7	9	5	10	5	10	5	10	5	12	6	12	5
POUTING	2½	2	2½	2	2½	2	3	2	2½	2	2½	2	3	2	2½	2	2¼	2	3	1¾
SCAD	1½	1	1½	1	1½	1	1	1	1½	1	1	1½	1½	1	1½	1	1½	1	1½	1
SHARK (BLUE)	40	–	40	–	40	–	40	–	40	–	40	–	40	–	40	–	85	–	100	–
SHARK (MAKO)	40	–	40	–	40	–	40	–	40	–	40	–	40	–	40	–	40	–	200	–
SHARK (POR BEAGLE)	40	–	40	–	80	–	80	–	80	–	80	–	80	–	75	–	175	–	175	–
SHARK (THRESHER)	40	–	40	–	40	–	40	–	40	–	40	–	40	–	40	–	100	–	150	–
RAY (BLONDE)	10	5	10	5	15	10	15	10	15	10	15	10	20	10	20	10	20	12	25	20
RAY (STING)	15	10	10	10	20	15	20	15	20	15	25	20	25	20	25	15	25	20	30	25
RAY (SMALL EYED OR PAINTED)	8	5	8	5	8	5	8	5	8	5	8	5	8	5	10	5	9	5	8	5
RAY (THORN-BACK)	13	8	12	5	17	12	15	12	17	12	15	12	15	12	15	12	15	12	15	12
SMOOTHOUNDS	12	5	10	5	13	10	15	10	13	10	13	10	13	10	15	10	5	3	20	15
SPUR DOG	10	5	10	5	12	8	15	8	12	8	10	8	10	8	10	8	5	3	12½	8
SOLE	2	2	2	2	1½	1½	2	2	1½	1½	1½	1½	1½	1½	2	2	2	2	1½	2
TOPE	30	15	20	15	35	30	35	30	35	30	40	30	40	30	35	28	40	30	45	45
TURBOT	12	7	10	4	15	7	15	5	15	7	10	7	10	7	12	7	10	6	19	9
WEAVER	¾	¾	¾	¾	¾	¾	¾	¾	1	1	1½	1	1½	1	¾	¾	¾	¾	¾	¾
WHITING	4	2	4	2	3	2	3½	2	3	2	2½	1	2½	1	2¾	1¾	2	1	3½	2
WRASSE	3	3	3	3	3	3	4½	4½	3½	3½	3	3	3	3	3½	3	5	5	5	5